Shattered

How God Transformed My Heart And Life

Judy Hehr

Contents

Acknowledgements

Glory to God for His unconditional love, infinite mercy, and amazing grace.

I want to thank my incredible husband, Bob, for staying and fighting for our family, for becoming a Godly man, for supporting me in every aspect of our family values. Thank you for parenting with me as we continue giving up what we want now for what we want most: to raise our children so that they never doubt God's love and plan for them, and that they don't repeat the cycles of defeat that we did. Thank you for your willingness to be transparent and share our story for the sake of others. I am so grateful for our tried, tested, and proven love. I would change nothing about our life!

To my children for always being so much stronger, confidant, wiser, and more faithful than I ever was. Thank you for every time you called me to more, for forgiving me for parenting out of my own brokenness, and for allowing this book to be available to bring hope to others.

To my mom and dad who never gave up on me, prayed for me continually, and became the most reliable confidants during the most difficult time in my life.

For every person before, during, and after the transformation of my life; for your presence, your prayers, and for your example, and your belief that my future could be bigger than my past.

For my siblings who loved me and were so concerned for me that you took measures that only make sense in retrospect.

For the Retrouvaille ministry, the Church, and the countless people who were "Jesus with skin" to me.

For Patti Maguire Armstrong who wrote this book and allowed what I experienced to be articulated in a way that is moving and meaningful and authentic to who I was and what God has done.

And for my friend and prayer partner Beth Struck who designed the cover.

Introduction

My greatest longing has always been to love and be loved.

So my journey of faith began with looking for love in all the wrong places. I sought attention, approval, and affirmation from people, places and things, not from God. I was on a desperate search for significance and to know that my existence mattered. I longed to belong and to be enough.

My journey has taken me from the highest highs to the lowest lows, and I have learned that there is nowhere that God will not go. My heart was broken piece by piece due to circumstances as well as choices that were both in and out of my control.

My heart was restless, and as Saint Augustine said to God "You have made us for yourself and our hearts are restless until they find rest in you." My desperate attempt and search for fulfillment, like Augustine, only proved to be a distraction and lead me further away from God.

As I continued to build my testimony and put a period and the end of my story as if it was over, God in his relentless pursuit of my soul, made every period a comma and waited patiently as the perfect gentleman He is, for me to love Him and let Him love me back.

I was lost, and I was in pain for so long: A homeless, drug addicted, abused, college dropout, who was bankrupt then became a millionaire and a mother of four. I achieved and attained everything that the world said would bring fulfillment. Yet, a heart remains restless until it rests in God.

God in His infinite love, gave me the greatest gift of letting my marriage implode and shattering my already broken heart into fifty million pieces. In His infinite grace and mercy He picked up every piece and restored it in such a way that it feels and loves like never before.

Now I know who I am and to whom I belong. I know that I matter and that I always was enough! I am a wife to my wonderful husband Bob, and a mother to my four amazing children Carter, Chandler, Kennedy, and Kampbell. In my professional life, I am an author, speaker, radio host, and leadership coach. But my truest identity lies in the fact that I am a Child of God. And that is enough!

I believe that unshared pain is wasted pain, and I pray that my story brings encouragement and hope to others. God has made it that my history has become my destiny. I want everyone to know that God's love has no bounds and His mercy and grace are always available.

May you read this and know that you are not alone.

Chapter 1
Self-Absorbed

This story is the perception of my life, my God, and myself. Although my siblings may have viewed things from a different perspective, perception is reality, and this was mine.

I had great parents who did the best they could with what they had and loved the way they knew how. My childhood seemed ideal from the outside looking in. I grew up with both parents, the fifth of six children in a Catholic family. Both my parents had alcoholic fathers, so they were deeply committed to giving their kids what they did not have—especially stability. They were intent on not repeating the cycles of defeat they experienced. My parents both lived their lives for their children, and they displayed their love in different ways.

My father focused on being a good provider. He never wanted his wife to struggle like his mother did. My dad worked a lot and found great satisfaction and significance in the success he achieved. He started out as a door-to-door salesman, eventually making his way up the ranks to become a division president of a Fortune 500 company. Respect mattered a lot to him. "I don't care if you like me," my dad often said, "but you will respect me." He demanded and deserved respect.

My mother never worked outside the home. Her job was to take care of us, and she loved doing that—perhaps too much. My dad once said, "I went from being number one when I married your mom to being in the number seven spot after all the children were born."

Like a typical traditional family, my father was the disciplinarian and my mother nurtured. It was the classic home life and both my parents did exactly what they believed they should to be a good parent.

There were sometimes situations when my parents had different parenting styles—Mom indulging and easy, and Dad stricter—yet I do not recall outward disagreements. It seemed they never fought. Since my dad was often out of town for work, when he came home, we put our best foot forward rather than rehash problems that had occurred during the week.

I wanted to walk a straight line and I craved attention for doing good things. I did not crave God, however. I did not have a relationship with Him. Looking back, I realize that I misunderstood a lot of things, which affected who I perceived God to be.

For instance, I remember asking Mom why Dad didn't go up for communion at Mass. She told me, "He feels he's unworthy." *Why would my hardworking, sacrificing Dad, who doesn't do anything wrong, be unworthy to receive communion?* I wondered. As an adult, my father clarified that if he was not in a state of grace and did not go to confession, he would not receive communion.

My parents fulfilled our Catholic duties and responsibilities. We never missed Sunday Mass or a holy day of obligation. I received the sacraments and was schooled in the practice of the faith, although not in Holy Scripture. Yet, I lacked an understanding of who God actually was.

My parents entrusted the upbringing of my faith to the Catholic school we attended. I do not recall ever talking about God outside of church. We were required to be present for family dinners, and they always started with grace and going around the table saying something we were grateful for. However, I never developed a personal relationship with Jesus at this time. Nor did the teachings of Scripture collide with the practice of my religion.

My perception of *my* faith and *my* God was like: *If you do that, God is going to punish you.* God was far away, distant, and condemning. This policeman-truant officer kind of God certainly was not a God I could turn to, draw strength from, or believe could be the source of all good things. I could never measure up.

I am not blaming my parents. They were heroic trying to provide a loving, nurturing, faith-filled home, and they far exceeded their own upbringing. They gave what they had with the most sincere intention and in the right spirit.

If my parents were the Bible, Dad would be Old Testament. He was all about the law: respect, obedience and discipline. Mom was New Testament. She was love, mercy, and forgiveness. I had the appearance of a good Catholic daughter, but I do not ever recall the message that I was a child of God.

I never felt that I fit in my family — not in the way my siblings did. I felt like something was lacking or missing. I was disengaged, disconnected, and irrelevant. I didn't feel loved, accepted, or connected. That is what I remember most about my childhood. So while my parents might have been thinking I was loved and nurtured, I felt rejected and dismissed.

I heard what was wrong and never what was right. It does not mean that was what was always said; it is just what I *heard*. That was the lens through which I viewed my childhood.

I do not have a really vivid memory of my childhood, and maybe that in itself is a gift from God. I can tell you that for as long as I can remember I had a constant feeling of discontent, longing, and lacking. I do not recall a time where I did not feel those feelings. Since birth, I have been pretty preoccupied with myself. I have learned that even a negative preoccupation is still a preoccupation. It is still rooted in pride. That is the way it has always been with me. It has always been all about me.

I had this sense of entitlement, of wanting more than I thought I was getting. In my report cards, teachers consistently stated over the years, "Judy needs more attention than I can give her. And she walks away when she feels neglected."

I was different, so I needed to stand out. I assumed the role of being the "good child" and that worked for a long time, until they absolutely loathed me because I was sure to measure myself by what they were not. I tried to show everyone how good I was, but really I was just pointing out how good they were not. I was self-righteous like Joseph (you know, Joseph and the coat of many colors). I judged I was better than my siblings, and I did what I needed to get the attention I craved. That just fostered further alienation from the support system and the family unit that I desperately longed for. That unfilled longing for attention continued to grow in me, so I felt dismissed and rejected, which caused behaviors that only made things worse.

There is darkness in my memory; things I would rather not remember. There were instances of sexual abuse that furthered my feelings of insignificance. It was done by people in authority that should have been forming my Catholic identity. As a child I did not know how to digest, sort out, explain, and deal with what had happened to me. I felt that I must have been bad — done something to deserve this.

I began feeling more insignificant, more irrelevant, more unworthy, and now very unclean, so that is what I became. I did not know the dignity of being a child of God.

My mother tried. She did the best she could to help me shape my identity, no matter how weak and fragile it was. I had an eating disorder—an attempt to be in control when I felt out of control. And at the height of my eating disorder, when a morsel of food would not stay in my body for ten minutes before I found a bathroom, Mom was the one who stood me in front of a mirror. With tears streaming down her face, she pleaded with me. "What do you see? What is wrong?" she cried. "What am I not seeing that you are seeing that is making you behave this way?"

I wish I could have said, *I just want to matter, Mom. I just want to be significant. I just want to be loved. I just want this hole in my soul to be filled with something.* But I did not know how to say that or how to say anything to make her understand.

That was how I first became a slave. I became controlled by my eating disorder, to my fears, and to my silence. Any studies done on eating disorders will tell you it is all about control. I could not control my feelings of worthlessness. I could not control my feelings of insignificance. But I could control *that.* And my way of feeling better about myself was to judge everyone else. It was an attempt to heal every wound that had ever been inflicted upon me. And it actually worked on the surface. But then everything fell apart and I could not pretend any longer.

For eighteen years I was able to stand on what I thought was the right thing. I was the "good child," a role that I had perfected. I did not do what my peers were doing. I did not want to be like them—I wanted to be better. Until I was eighteen, I did not drink or use drugs. I did not engage in what I believed to be inappropriate behavior. I did all the right things, and I let others know about the wrong things they were doing. That is how I made myself feel better. Until, that is, it was not enough.

Chapter 2
Self-Pity

My mother was the rock; she was always there. When I needed her, she was there. When I brought my friends home, at school functions and sporting events, she was there—to cater to me, to do whatever I needed her to do.

Then, during my senior year of high school, my mother dropped dead unexpectedly of a heart attack. It completely rocked my world. She had not even been sick. There was no warning. She just *died* of a heart attack. The "heart" of our family was gone. She was there one moment and gone the next.

I remember vividly coming home from school and Mom was sitting in a chair. She said she was not feeling well. "But my friends are here and we're hungry," I said. It was about me, and I was worried about my own plans. It always seemed like my mom would just be able to meet whatever my needs and wants were. I never once considered her needs. She lived for us. Period.

Dad was out of town on a business trip, so a neighbor came over. Mom got into his car, and he drove her to the hospital. My younger brother and I followed to the hospital in our car, arguing over who was going to stay with Mom because we both had plans that night.

When we got to the hospital, someone came out to talk to us. "We tried everything, but she didn't make it," we were told.

What? I could not comprehend what that meant. I heard the words, but they would not sink in. We could not live without my mom. *This can't and isn't happening! It is not possible for her to be gone.*

I called my dad, just going through the motions on autopilot. "Dad, you need to come home. Now! Mom died," I must have said.

It was March 17, 1984 and she was only fifty-four years old. My siblings all gathered at the hospital. I did not even know how everyone got there. Then my dad showed up in businessman mode, not like a man who had just lost his wife. We were all in shock. How could there be life without my mother in it?

Through the funeral and the days afterward, I still felt nothing. It wasn't right. But how can you make yourself start feeling? There was a vast emptiness where my mother used to be. I loved her so much, but I do not think I ever stopped to feel that when she was with us. If I thought about how much I loved her at that point, it would feel too late. My mother was not there to love anymore, so I could only miss her and that could only mean a bottomless pit of pain. And regret. If only I had been given the chance to say good-bye. If only I had known I was never going to see her again, I could have loved her with everything I had. Just like she had loved me. But it was too late.

The house was full of people, but I felt alone and isolated. I felt no connection to my siblings while preparing for my mom's funeral. I was concerned most about my little brother. He was Mom's favorite and the baby of the family and was already struggling with issues of his own. Yet, we grieved in a way that only distanced us from one another.

One sibling said, "Well, now you can have Dad all to yourself; you don't have to share him with Mom." Although I did not think so at the time, years later, my siblings told me that I had always been dad's favorite.

My mother had held everything in our family together. She tried to instill faith into us. She went to church, and, of course, she loved God. Mom was always doing good for others. So why was she gone? No one told me, "God's ways are not our ways. He works all things for good for those who love Him." Although, such words might not have mattered to me then.

What God would take away a mother like mine? Mom was my tangible image of Christ. She was a mother to six children and a grandmother. God stole her from me. He no longer existed as far as I was concerned. It was so painful. I did not know what to do with that pain so I buried it, afraid to feel the depth of whom and what I had lost.

A tree with strong roots weathers any storm. I had no roots and my foundation was built on sand. Everything quickly washed away once my mother was no longer there to give me support. Everything was gone and buried with her.

In the limousine on the way to the funeral, Dad called my attention to the line of cars with their lights on stretching behind us as far as I could see. "Look how many people's lives your mother touched," he said.

It isn't fair! was all I could think. This was my senior year of high school. Mom would not be there for my prom, spring break, graduation, college, and someday my wedding. It hurt me then, and even now it still does, that she would not be there for the birth of my children or be involved in their lives. My pain was buried so deeply that even today, I do not think I have fully mourned her loss.

I was filled with resentment toward my siblings. They had Mom for all of that. Self-pity filled me. And changed me. The girl who always did everything right, suddenly stopped feeling. Anything.

I was not going to be better than everyone else any more. What difference did it make if I had to walk alone? I was soon to start walking paths I had never gone before.

Although I had received a sports scholarship that year and could have gone away to college, I chose to stay home and go to the community college thinking I could take care of my father. I wanted to fill in the gap my mother had left. But I couldn't be her. I did not even

17

know where to begin. My dad was there physically, but he was lost emotionally. He just seemed so lost and sad. I tried to do the things my mom had done, but I could not even do the little things like just make dinner.

I remember once Dad tried to make dinner. He tried to fry an egg on a flat pan, but it did not work. He just stood there and cried. Until that moment, I had never realized the magnitude of my mother's presence in our family. She had done and been everything for all of us.

Mom

Chapter 3
Condemnation

Death can do one of two things to a family: it can bring them together or drive them apart. Unfortunately, my mother's death did not bring me closer to my family. Dad did the best he could, but he was distant and dealing with his own pain. He did not understand what I was doing or where I was at in my life. He was not equipped to be a mother to me. I became distant from God and everything connected with Him. Although my grandmother ministered to me and taught me how to do things around the house, it was not the same. Nothing would ever be the same without my mom; not ever.

My goal became to stop the pain. Before my mother died, there had been pain and confusion, but now it was like the lid blew off. I had only turned eighteen on March 8. Her birthday was March 13, she turned fifty-four, and then she died on March 17, St. Patrick's Day–with only three months left before high school graduation. Everything is different when you know the person who loved you the most in the whole world was not going to show up for anything. Ever again.

That summer I was eighteen, feeling unsought, uncertain and unseen. There was no hope. My mother was not coming back. I started hanging out with different friends whose values and upbringings were unlike my own—ones that liked partying and drinking. I was working at a fitness center, teaching aerobic classes and selling memberships. The owners introduced me to cocaine and it was love at first snort.

Within a year, I dropped out of the community college, (although I had told so many people over the years that I had a two-year degree, that I believed it myself). I started to fill the hole in my soul with everything I swore I never would do: smoking, drinking, drugs, and promiscuous behavior. If it felt good, I did it. If it made the pain go away, it must be good. And I have to say, it made a difference. For those periods of time when I did not have to be in my own skin, it was okay. It numbed the pain.

My dad was not happy with my new friends and told me, "You're judged by the company you keep." He would not condone or support my destructive behavior. He told me that he was not going to stand by and see my gifts and talents not being utilized. I had to stop it or leave home.

In the meantime, my dad had found someone new in his life, Anita, and remarried. She was and is an amazing woman who, today, I consider one of my closest confidants and support system. She knew I was doing drugs and had an eating disorder. She tried desperately to save me and convinced my father something was drastically wrong. She and my dad tried to get through to me, but I was so far gone. Although I honestly hated the pain I was causing them, I could not stop. The constant hurt and disappointment were too much to bear. I swore things would be different. Every time I would promise no more lies, no more drugs, no more episodes, but it only continued. I despised who I was and what I had become.

I saw them as judgmental and condemning; clearly they didn't get it. So I moved from my upper middle class residence to a roach-infested apartment in a bad part of town. It was all I could afford. Emotionally, it cost me more than I wanted to pay.

The fitness center had fired me since I had become unethical and unreliable. I began waitressing and working at Macy's department store. It was not long before I was fired from Macy's for stealing. I worked on commission. I would convince friends to come in and buy something and then return it at another Macy's store in another part of town, so that when they got their money back at that store, I could still keep the commission. It was not long before the management figured out what was going on.

When my dad came to visit me, he cried. "Why do you want to live here when you can live at home?" He was heartbroken and confused. I was out of control and there was nothing he could do to stop it.

But I was not going to give up my lifestyle. It was how I dealt with—or didn't deal with—the pain I was in. The amount, duration, and selection of drugs magnified. By then I was doing speed, cocaine, alcohol, and marijuana. I hung around some scary people, and they made me feel better about me because I wasn't as bad as them—at least not at first.

Partying eventually wears thin. The self-destructive behaviors led to despair, hopelessness, and powerlessness. I had eroded my God-given dignity, but I did not understand that was where the pain was coming from. I did not even think about God. Why would I even want that punishing God? My goal in life was just to be numb, to not feel. I just lived for the moment. I had no realization of how I was hurting others through my sin. I understand now that sin is not an isolated an event.

The feelings of self-pity grew into self-condemnation. I lived in that self-made pit for five years. There are three things that constitute a pit: you cannot stand, you feel stuck, and you lose vision. Your pit does not have to be as bad as mine, but that is what constitutes one. I do not care if you got thrown into your pit, if you slipped into your pit, or if, like me, you dug your pit yourself and jumped in; it is a pit all the same. Pits can get very comfortable. Mine did. I got comfortable and made myself at home.

Baggage attracts baggage. It is part of being comfortable. I kept company with a lot of people who were just like me. If they were not, I made sure to drag them down. I was especially attracted to people worse than me. It was an opportunity to feel superior. *At least I am not that bad,* I would think. I had a lot of friends then, but no one ever encouraged me to stop the destructive behavior. But how could they? They were in the pit with me. This was my life and I did not see it ever changing. I was ready to put a period at the end of my story. Instead, God was putting in a comma.

Maybe God had sent someone to be a significant Christ-like example for me, but, if they were there, I did not see them. I would have rejected them to continue living my new "normal." My dad and my new mom tried to get me out of the pit, but what did they know? They would never understand. They had moved on and had a new life together. I was making a mess of my own life and wreaking havoc on theirs whenever they tried to help me.

If you spell—s-i-n—the center is always *I*. That is what my life revolved around—me. It was always self-serving, not life-giving. My partying friends and I were not donating our money to the poor or doing anything to help make anyone's life better. But sin has a price and it cost me way more than I ever expected to pay. I became spiritually and emotionally bankrupt.

It finally got to the point that I wanted to change my life, but I had no idea how. How do you find dignity when you are so disgusted with what you have become? Self-pity had become self-hatred. I broke every commandment countless times. I killed my conscience and viewed everything in a deformed way. But I was sick and tired of being sick and tired. I was ready to start over.

Our wedding day!

Chapter 4
Preservation

I got into some trouble, and I owed a lot of people money—scary people. Someone had threatened to hurt my father if I did not pay him. Those were the kind of people I was in involved with. I had good reason to be fearful for myself and possibly for my dad.

It was humiliating to put my family in danger because of my decisions and choices. I needed to get away, but I did not know how or where to go. Thank God (although I would not have thanked Him then) for my grandmother. Although she knew I was in trouble, my grandmother did not realize the extent of it. She was always there to help us when we could not seem to help ourselves. She was not afraid to face my problems. She was aware of my addiction to drugs and wanted to help. She gave me money, and in the middle of the night, helped me to pack up whatever could fit in my Plymouth Turismo, and sent me to Chicago where my three sisters lived.

I just disappeared from my life as I knew it and headed toward a clean slate and a new beginning by using a geographical cure. And guess what I found when I arrived? More baggage. Because wherever you go, there *you* are.

I found myself doing the same things and expecting different results. I continued being promiscuous, drinking, and doing drugs. My new life became my old life. I moved in with an old friend and her parents, but she told me, "No drugs, drinking, or funny business if you live here."

I did not follow the rules. "You are off the rails," she told me one day. "This isn't fun anymore—it's a problem."

For a period of time, I hooked up with people, crashed on their couches, stayed with one friend and then another, or when no one would put me up, I slept in my car. I could have been considered homeless, which by definition is displaced, destitute, and down-and-out. I had no home to call my own. How had I fallen this far?

I was so high and full of lies so much of the time that I do not remember what my plan was then, but I knew I wanted to be dead. It seemed like the best option for all concerned. The thought of life without drugs was unimaginable, but life with drugs was clearly not an option. There was no hope for me.

On a Sunday morning at 4:00 a.m., I found the courage to call the suicide hotline. "Please hold," the stranger's voice said. I could not believe it! I was calling out for help because I wanted to kill myself, and I was put on hold! This further validated my sense of worthlessness. Yet, I waited. What did I have to lose?

When the stranger came back on the line, I spoke. "I think I need some help." The voice on the other end of the line told me to go to a treatment center on Monday morning for an evaluation. So much for emergency help. I do not know how, but I made it through Sunday to Monday morning. I did not really want to die; I just wanted to stop hurting. My best friend Mary Kay went with me to the treatment center for the evaluation.

I signed and was committed to receive help at the treatment center, but I was completely consumed with fear. *What if I fail? How can I live without drugs or alcohol?*

The counselor (who called me the wrong name for the next twelve weeks, which certainly did not help my identity) looked me in the eye and said, "It is now time to be honest. When was the last time you drank?"

"On the way here."

"When was the last time you did other drugs?"

"Today"

He looked disgusted and abruptly closed up the file. "This eval is over," he said. "This program is about abstinence."

Absti...-what? I swear, I thought they were going to teach me how to be normal— how to do this like a normal person. I knew people who could do these things normally. They ate normally. They drank normally. They smoked normally. But I did not think I was normal. I was *never* the normal one. I looked up at him anxiously, dumbfounded.

"You can go home now," he said.

Fear shot through me. My heart pounded. *What would become of me?* I could not keep getting high, but I could not *not* keep getting high. I pleaded for help.

He looked at me and said, "If you sign right here," (I had no money, so I had to sign a note) "we will trust that you are going to obey the rules of this program. If you do not, you are out!"

Fear continued to grip me. How could I ever live in this skin without something to numb me? Now, more than ever, I needed it to hide from my life and all the shameful things I had done and who I had become.

I had no coping skills and certainly no feelings, because I had numbed them for as long as I could remember. This newness felt raw and uncomfortable, and I was so incredibly tempted to talk myself back into my safe, comfortable pit.

In treatment, there were only a handful of people who were willing to share deeply. I felt resentful. Even though I had signed up for help, I did not trust them. I was never going to share. I would show them; I wouldn't give them anything.

28

"Admit that your life is unmanageable," they said. "Get yourself a Higher Power."

In treatment, I was reintroduced to this God. He was going to help me. He was going to help me stay clean and sober if I turned my life and my will over to Him every day. *Yeah, right.* I had no dignity. I had no character.

"When you obey God, look for the things He shows you instantly, because instantly a door opens," they said. Well, that was good to know. Instant gratification, I understood. I expected to see some really quick results, or I was out of there.

I know now the cross is a plus sign and suffering is redemptive. I learned what the power of the cross really provided: either to be delivered from something or be given the strength to endure. On July 10, 1989, God removed my overwhelming need and desire to use drugs

As cynical and untrusting as I was, hope began to enter my life. I wanted to succeed, but I did not tell that to very many people. I usually failed, so I did not want to make anyone any promises; not even to myself.

I invited my family to come to the sessions and one of them came. The other two had their own lives, and I have come to understand that you can't give what you don't have. Every day I would wake up and say, *I am not going to do this anymore. I do not want to live this way anymore.* And I prayed to God that I would be right.

I guess I would say that I was given healing, even though I had still not come to know the Healer. My changes did not last very long, however, because nothing outside changes for very long until we change inside.

My problem was less about giving love to God than it was about receiving it. How could He love me? How could I ask Him to love that which I hated? I struggled with shame, guilt, and blame. Yet, I kept hearing in my head: "I know the plans I have for you, plans to prosper you, plans to give you a future and a hope," (Jeremiah 29:11).

In treatment, I learned that I was only as sick as my secrets. We keep our secrets and our secrets keep us. I was pretty sick. I know that Scripture says, "Those who are well do not need a physician." I was not well. I needed something. Desperately.

When I completed treatment, on graduation day, the message was not very encouraging to me. Everyone receives a letter from those in treatment with them. It was meant to be written as inspiration, something you could take with you and pull out to re-read when you needed strength. Here is what my letters said:

You'll never make it.

Good luck – you've got a long road.

You hide behind your humor.

You wear too many masks.

You'll never stay clean and sober.

Even worse than those letters, the counselor added a psychological evaluation that identified the following:

- ❖ Chronically poor judgment
- ❖ Overly critical and unpredictable
- ❖ Resentful
- ❖ Emotionally isolated
- ❖ Standing still in life
- ❖ Confused and scattered thoughts
- ❖ Trust and intimacy issues

He went on to reiterate my defects of character: defensive, critical, jealous, sarcastic, impatient, compulsive, and self-conscious. In summary he stated, "You have a 98% chance of never being able to stay clean and sober." He did not think I had dealt with the things that had driven me to my addicted behavior.

I dismissed them and their opinions. I had done this. I had gone through this twelve-week treatment. I did it! That meant something to me. I did what they told me to do, and I was clean and sober. Still, the fear I had gone in with came out with me. I had no education. I had no skills to speak of that were not demoralizing and degrading; however, I had a genuine desire for my life to change—more than I wanted it to stay the same. I know never to underestimate the power of desire.

I made a dinner date with my father to tell him that I was clean and sober. This was significant. I told him I was finally ready to be responsible. But he was not happy for me; he was sad.

"You were made for so much more than this," he said. "You have all these gifts, but you are not using any of them." Dad had a vision of what I could be. I had often been referred to as his favorite, but I had disappointed him. He made it clear that he expected so much more; he would not accept mediocrity. I felt judged but I still had a lot to learn and to feel. Today, I realize as I parent our children, that I want to convey those same messages to them.

Before I went into treatment, my oldest sister and her husband had offered to help me get back on my feet, although she had her own family and responsibilities. "We'll tell you what," they had said. "You get yourself into a treatment center and you can stay with us." *Treatment?* I thought. Who needs treatment? *I have this all under control.* But after admitting they were right and getting the help I so desperately needed, I ended up moving in with them for a period of time. They helped me tremendously. While living with them I had accountability, a family atmosphere, and great guidance emotionally, spiritually, and financially.

Without them opening their home and hearts, I am uncertain that I could have stayed clean.

I had so much to work on, so many defects of character, and still a long road to recovery.

Chapter 5
Importance

I graduated from treatment, despite the odds. Sobriety became my focus. I did what was recommended in order to stay clean. I attended meetings daily, worked the 12 Steps and found a sponsor. I knew I was powerless and turned my life and will over to God. I found deliverance and strength in my recovery. I wanted so much to be self-aware and face the demons of my past—what I had done and who I had become. I was working the 12 Steps of AA and working toward doing the fourth step. It requires taking "a searching and fearless moral inventory." The goal was to learn and know myself, accept myself, and then to start applying it to my daily life. I discovered so many areas where I needed to change. I was able to be honest for the first time in a long time. It became glaringly obvious there were plenty of areas that needed to be addressed. Perfectionism, putting others down, and admitting mistakes, became more difficult as I was unable to blame it on drug use any more. It was difficult to be myself as I struggled with getting past the past, patience in the area of my progress in recovery just to name a few. Although the road ahead seemed long, I desperately wanted my life to change.

Any desire for that old life regarding completely left me. This was the first time I had profoundly felt God's presence in a very long time, and it became something that I really needed and relied on to get my life back on track. There was no other explanation other than God, as this was the first time in a long time I had reason to hope. I believed it had to be God who removed my desire to use drugs and alcohol.

The "Serenity Prayer" became very important to me. It was simple and made sense to me. I said it often. This reintroduction to God had flaws, however. My desire was fueled by fear as opposed to faith. This was a God for calling on in desperation. I depended on Him to stay sober. Granted, it was a conversion, but not yet a transformation. I had so much to face up to and admit to regarding what I had done and who I had become. My heart was still a stone.

Naturally, I was told in treatment to stay away from bars. I got a job in one right away. I was not ignoring the advice I had received, but I owed a $10,000 debt for the treatment itself. Plus, I still owed a lot of people money. Tending bar was my best option for income given I had no particular skill set.

A gentleman named Joe Witry used to come in on a regular basis. He owned a printing broker business. There was an aura of importance about him, and his salespeople always surrounded him. Although I did not know much about him, I knew he was influential and successful.

"You can be making a lot of money," he said to me one day, after I had worked at the bar for a couple of months. "Why are you here doing this? You are wasting your ability. You can be successful."

I laughed it off. *Hey, I am successful. You have no idea! I am clean and sober. I am going to meetings, working the 12 Steps of AA and NA, and I am making $200 a week bartending!*

"You do not understand," I said. "I need this job. I have no skills. I have no money."

I did not take him seriously, but Joe persisted. "You are going to work for me, and you are going to make a lot of money," he said.

A lot of money? He had my attention. "What exactly would I be doing?" I asked. He told me I would be selling printing. Printing? What did I know about printing?

"I have no doubt you can do it. You're the best!" he said, "I will pay you $200 a week." I thought he was crazy. He was offering to pay me the same amount I was making at the bar, except I had no skills, no training, and no experience. I thought it was a joke, yet there was something about him that seemed genuine.

When I told my father about the offer, he thought it was a scam. He flew out to meet this person. We had dinner together, and my dad asked a million questions. Although he was not entirely convinced that I would make a lot of money, he decided that Joe was legitimate.

Joe was actually a person who could see ability in people, and he thrived on providing opportunities for people to change their lives—to have a future bigger than their past. He was willing to take a chance with people who had less than desirable histories. I was honest about my past. He saw my obstacles as opportunities and knew my future could be bigger than my past. No other companies would have hired me. The promise of unbridled success was before me. I was never motivated by money; I was motivated by Joe's belief in me despite my past.

I was so grateful for the opportunity to have a future that was not held back by my past. Joe told me that I had what it took to be a great salesperson. I took him at his word. The majority of the other salespeople were twice my age, and I was the first and only woman who ever worked for him as a salesperson.

We were his protégées. Joe hired people out of the most unusual situations. He would go out and find people for what they could be and not necessarily what they were. He hired people randomly as he came across them. He saw in others what no one else did.

He told his salespeople, "Do what I tell you to do and how to do it, and you will be successful." We were. It was about connecting with people and building relationships.

Ironically, in the printing business, it is important to understand sizes. To this day, I cannot read a ruler. I knew nothing about the business, but I jumped in and got started.

My starting paying was $200 a week. Although that is not a lot, keep in mind that in 1989, $200 had the buying power that $600 has today. Joe allowed me to keep my bartending job because I needed to make more money than he was paying me. His salespeople worked on straight commissions.

The first week I worked for Joe, I got arrested for driving without a license. I called him and said, "Thanks anyway, but this obviously is not going to work." It was such a hard phone call for me to make. I added, "I am sorry that I let you down."

Instead of letting me go, Joe sent me back to New Jersey with a wad of cash and said, "You clear up everything that is out there. Come back here with a valid driver's license. Remember, you're the best!"

A couple of weeks went by and the mantra expanded, "You're the best, but you have to look successful to be successful." He sent me to Fashion Bug with another wad of cash. I had the biggest shopping spree of my life. I spent $500. I understood that I had to look successful to be successful.

Then he came to me and said again, "You have to look successful to be successful." He took me to a car dealership. I had been driving what I thought was a perfectly good Plymouth Turismo. It got me where I needed to go. It was enough for me, but I believed in what Joe was saying. I needed to look successful to be successful.

Joe made it clear that the money was not a gift but an investment. He told me that I would make enough money to pay him back for all the upfront costs of getting me established. It was an investment and I actually did soon pay it back.

I did what Joe said because he was the first person who believed in me since my life had spiraled out of control. I had been very unpredictable and unreliable, not to mention untrustworthy. Everything he told me permeated every part of my being. He gave me a chance. Nobody else had. Until Joe.

When I first started, I was selling to small businesses. Before too long, I walked into Fortune 500 companies confident that I could establish a connection and save them money. I was in the office at 6:00 a.m., out in the field by 8:00 a.m., and back in the office at 4:00 p.m. to do follow up. I did everything Joe told me to do. I sold printing, promotional products, and anything I could provide for my customers. I had never done anything like this in my life. I put all my trust in this man and did whatever he told me to do. He said, "You just wear them down." And I did.

I worked the way I had done drugs and everything else for that matter—over the top. That was me. The answer *no* was just another reason to get them to say *yes*. My personality is to put my entire being into whatever I am doing—two-hundred percent. ALL IN!

I worked with fifty men. Fifty men and me. I was twenty-three and most of these men were middle-aged. They had to have all been wondering what rock I had crawled out from under. But after all, that is where Joe found a lot of us, from under rocks and other odd places.

He saw potential, and said, "Follow me." He was like Jesus, but with this guy you could keep your possessions and actually measure your worth by expanding them. I liked this guy's options. They worked for me.

I hung onto his every word and did exactly what he said. Then, he made mention of something that confused me. "You are going to pay more in taxes your second year than you made your first year in income."

I called my dad, because I had no idea what this meant exactly. "It means he is lying, because that would be impossible," my Dad said. I ignored his words and continued to do what Joe told me to do.

After the first year working for Joe, he announced that I was going on straight commission. The long and short of it is that everything he said was going to happen, happened. In my eleven-year career, I was the top salesperson in the country, a millionaire by age thirty, selling $75 million worth of product. All of it was based on sizes, and I really did not even know how to read a ruler. For me, things kept coming together over and over and over. I was making more money than anyone could ever imagine. Achieving, accumulating, accomplishing, and attaining drove my life at that point.

Success, right? But it became my new form of slavery. My new addiction was success. Although my new addiction was healthier and much more socially acceptable, I still heard a voice saying, "You cannot serve two masters. If you love one, you will hate the other." That same voice whispered, "What good is it to gain the whole world if you lose your soul?" I pushed those words away.

I was successful. I was important. I was large and in charge. When I spoke people listened. I had put God right back on the shelf. It was great that He got me clean and sober, but I was fine now. *I got this. I am back in control again.*

I congratulated myself for my own achievements. I did not need God. I built my own kingdom and lorded it over others. *See how important I am! Look what I have done and overcome.* The new self was self-important. I was that person who parked in the handicap spot. I am not handicapped. I was the one who walked into Starbucks where fifty people could be in line, and I would think to myself, *Hello! Maybe you don't recognize me but I am important! I am busy. I do not have time to stand in lines.*

I judged everyone as either inferior or superior to me. It decided who deserved my respect and who did not and took away their dignity at every turn. My favorite quote was, "God created the world in six days and rested on the seventh—make it happen." That was the only time I

mentioned God's name unless it was in vain. If anyone ever questioned
if I was religious at this time, I would clarify that I was not religious. I
called myself spiritual.

The beginning of our adventure

Chapter 6
Sacrifice

Self-entitlement robbed me of any appreciation of the blessings of God. Anything the good Lord gave me, including even my next breath, was of no credit to Him. I was driven by fear and pride, and my feelings were rooted in insecurity and uncertainty.

I felt important and my actions toward others led them to feel less than. For so long, I craved approval and acceptance, and I had arrived at having both. Sadly, I went overboard to the opposite extreme. I am not proud of the way I treated people in my path; it was not intentional. I believed I had "made it." It is only in looking back that I realize exactly how poorly I treated so many people.

I can only describe my thought pattern in hindsight. People around me have said I always had a big heart. That was true in one respect, but I also realize that I was always pushing to get ahead and putting people into categories as being either more or less than me.

St. Vincent De Paul said to judge others in the most favorable light at all times and in all circumstances. Unfortunately, we see things as we are, not as they are.

Before my mother died, my foundation was built on sand, so the person that I believed I was, quickly washed away. Now, I had built another house but on rocky soil. God and goodness could not take root. Instead my rocky foundation was:

❖ Driven by a false sense of self.

❖ A mistaken identity of who and whose I was.

❖ Not glorifying God or seeing His work in my life.

I thought I was doing fine without God. Rather than recognize that it is God who gives us our talents and abilities and opens the doors to possibilities, I took all the credit for myself.

The whole "look successful to be successful" mantra fostered a new pretense that was not so unlike the old one. As a matter of fact, it was the same pretense just with a different face.

- ❖ If it looks good, it must be good.
- ❖ If I look good, I must be good.
- ❖ If I look happy, I must be happy.

Riches cannot satisfy an empty soul, and possessions cannot fill a life void of purpose. The problem of "self" still haunted me. I had gone from self-pity, to self-hatred and self-condemnation, into self-importance.

I was freed from the bondage of drugs and alcohol, but I had even more pride, more position, more possessions, and more prayerlessness. My conscience was deformed and malformed. I was still a slave in bondage, this time to self-importance and moved to a place of self-justification.

Whatever happened to that little girl in the mirror who just wanted to love and be loved? She was still hiding and running. At that time, I had everything that the world said would bring fulfillment: a successful career, luxury home, expensive cars, the most expensive clothes and jewelry, and later, even a husband and four healthy children. I had absolutely everything money could buy. But not God. God was not for purchase, and I was not shopping for Him anyway.

So while I lived with my self-entitled, presumptuous, arrogant attitude and condescending treatment of those around me, I met Bob. Bob's father owned a company that was a vendor to my company. Bob came in to do a sales presentation and from the minute he walked into the room, I was drawn to him like a moth to a flame.

We had a business meeting over lunch and our conversation turned personal. I judged that his arrogance might be a façade. Yet, there was something about Bob that left me wanting more. I wanted to pull him in and push him away at the same time. After our lunch, I thought, "What a jerk. I hope he calls."

Bobby and I went on our first date November 7, 1992, got engaged January 9, and were married on August 28, 1993. Bob was everything that every other man was not. He elicited feelings in me that I did not know existed. He made me feel loved, accepted, safe, secure, and wanted. He gave me something that no other man ever had. He came into my life respecting me, empowering me, trusting me, and just loving me. *Just loving me.* That was very unfamiliar. Being with him fed the starving places in my soul. I believe Bob thought I had it all together, when really I could have so easily fallen apart.

I absolutely adored Bob and believed we were meant for one another. I felt complete, like I had finally found the missing piece of the puzzle. It was the first time in my life that I felt hopeful about being married and living happily ever after. I hung onto his every word as if it were gospel. My father referred to him as "Bobby Said," because often in conversation I would proclaim every word that "Bobby said."

Bob and I were married in the Catholic Church, not because it was important to me, but it was important to my parents. I was indifferent about where we got married. Together we went through Pre-Cana, a requirement prior to marriage in the Catholic Church, yet I don't recall it having prepared us for anything that we would face in the future.

We flippantly discussed things like our compatibility and the basic principles of Catholic marriage and family life. At our wedding, I remember kneeling in front of a statue of Mary, , during Mass and whispering under my breath, "How long do we have to stay here in front of this statue?" We really had no idea what it would take to have the union God intended. We went through the motions not knowing what would lie ahead by not inviting God to be the center of our union. I did not really "get" this union that was going to take place between two imperfect people or the necessity of God being an intricate part of it. I had no idea that Mary, the mother of Jesus, would later lead me to her Son and be the source of graces needed to navigate the most painful time of my life.

I will tell you, that based on the way I entered into sacraments—marriage being one of them—your disposition does matter. The sacraments are grace-filled and life changing when you come with open hands and an open heart. But when all you are filled with is yourself, there is no room for God and all He has to give. He can't fill us with Himself when we are already filled with our self. "God does not fit in an occupied heart," -St John of the Cross.

When I came to this marital union, I had a lifetime of unmet longings and unfulfilled desires. I was a broken person with a lot of baggage. True, it was now a Gucci bag instead of the old brown paper bag, but it was baggage nonetheless. I carried with me an empty bucket that screamed, "Fill me! Love me! Need me! Want me!" I thought Bob was going to fix everything.

After we got married, we moved into Bob's house. I had been living in a townhouse that I owned, but we moved into his. Then we built our first home together, on a golf course in Illinois. I allowed Bob into my inner circle, but before long, he would not be able to live up to my expectations either.

I kept working, making more money, and climbing the corporate ladder. My career was sailing, and I was building my kingdom. The bigger I became, the smaller Bob became. As I climbed higher, I was kicking Bob in the face. In essence, I was telling him, "I don't need you; I got this."

I emasculated my husband out of my own fear and pride. I took care of myself and could not let anyone control me. I struggled desperately with measuring up for Bob and others. It was as if I was in a contest with no other contestants, and I was determined to win. The standing joke between Bob and me became, "Can you just lower the bar?" I would like to say I threw the bar out, but I did not.

God blessed me with my first child; I saw Him in my son. But what was He thinking? How could something so pure come from something so defiled? Somebody said to me, "You'll probably be a really good mother for boys, but not so much for girls." I smiled and laughed it off, but deep down I wondered if they were right. What did I possibly know about being a mother to a child? I honestly thought that anyone would be more equipped than I was at motherhood. It made sense to go back to what I did best, which was work. I would let a professional take care of our child. I hired a nanny, and I went back to my career. I was important there. I was valued. I had business to attend to. People needed me. That was addicting.

I was so entitled that rules didn't apply to me. I just did what I wanted, when I wanted where I wanted. When I went into labor I was able to smoke in my hospital room – *while* I was delivering a child. My doctor made it clear since it was me it was ok. I was so important I was on the phone in the delivery room, and the doctor announced, "The baby's head is crowning, could you hang up now?" I was so very important.

I embraced motherhood by providing for my family monetarily. I went to work every day, and people would say, "You could never be a stay-at-home mom; you are way too driven." What I did not understand is that I could not be a stay-at-home mom because I felt I had nothing to give my children. I was an empty shell of a person who fed on the approval, the acceptance, and the affirmation of others. I found my satisfaction in my career, not in being a mom. After all, I was successful at work and had no proof of that being the case as a mom.

I went to work and was fed every day. I was constantly told how great I was, and I received substantial monetary compensation. I was salesperson of the year over and over and showered with attention and affirmation. People bent over backward to please me, and if they did not, I made sure that changed. I was large and in charge. The unreasonable expectations I had affected everyone, including my nanny. I would come home and tell the nanny, "Their nails are dirty," or "You are supposed to switch the toys out every six weeks...His hair is not combed, and why aren't they wearing matching shirts?" There was no such thing as mediocrity. Only perfection.

The things that I found fault in were so superficial and insignificant. Yet at the time they seemed monumental.

Honestly, at the time, I thought it acceptable since I was paying them, so I had the right to have my expectations met. I really, truly believed that. It never dawned on me until years later that with every interaction I took away dignity.

I worked and I worked and I worked. I worked until I delivered each one of our children. I worked, delivered a baby, and was on the phone before the end of the day. Once I had a business trip, and Bob decided to drive all of us as a family to Delaware in an RV. Did you know in a proper RV, you can nurse a child, cook a hot dog, and build a Lego set at the same time? I learned that this mothering thing was really hard work. There was no measurement of success and not much appreciation. No one said thank you. No one told me how great I was. No one told me how important I was.

People thought we had the perfect life and the perfect family—complete with cars, house, and vacations. But, while I was busy building my kingdom, my marriage was slowly eroding. When we saw our relationship began to struggle, Bob and I were wise enough to invest in the help of a therapist. We went diligently and sought tools to contribute to the health of our marriage. We were also confused why it seemed our kids were so intense and irritable. She later pointed out that they possessed the very characteristics of Bob and me.

I joked about how I would be able to blame any therapy my children ended up needing on their nanny, because clearly those were their formative years, and I was busy working. The little impact that I had cannot possibly have done that much damage, right? I did not get what was happening around me because of me.

I spent many years building my kingdom and my false sense of self. I had attained everything the world says brings fulfillment: a family, a home, a thriving career, and anything money could buy. But, as Saint Augustine said after he learned it for himself, "A heart remains restless until it rests in God."

I was restless. Like an itch that could never be scratched, my insatiable yearning to fill the hole in my soul continually left me raising the bar for myself as well as for others. No one met my expectations. Not my husband. Not my kids. Not my nanny. Nobody. Including myself. Somewhere in Scripture it says, "You look but you do not perceive and you hear but you do not understand[1]." That was me. The worst thing about thinking you are living for God is just *thinking* you are. I did. I *thought* I was doing all the right things. I was working hard and trying to be a good wife and mother. But nothing changed in my heart.

I know now that I could not get past the past. For a while I remembered how unworthy I was, and then I would remember how worthy (self-important) I was. It was always one extreme or the other.

If you do not love God, you will love anything. And I did.

After I had three children, I started working out and incorporating fitness into my daily life. It quickly became the next addiction. I worked out so much and achieved such unusual levels of fitness after childbirth

---

[1] Paraphrased from Matthew 13:13

that it got the attention of many. I was featured in national fitness magazines as an inspiration to others, especially mothers. People would say, "Do you realize how far you have come?" And I would say, "Yeah!" And I would think to myself, *Aren't I awesome? Aren't I amazing?* Looking back, it is so baffling that I could be so blind to God's hand at work in my life.

And I would think to myself, *Aren't I awesome? Aren't I amazing?* Looking back, it is so baffling that I could be so blind to God's hand at work in my life.

In late 2000, when we had three children—two boys and a little girl all under the age of five—I talked Bob into having one more child. Just one more. On the outside, it might not have made sense. If I was too busy for the ones we had, why would I want one more? But I did love them, and I longed for them in a way that I could not understand.

I just wanted one more baby—another opportunity to embrace pregnancy and the miracle of life as well as the maternity leave I never received. I promised Bob that this time, everything related to the kids would not default to him. I would make sacrifices. I would be there. Bobby was the one who had to stay home from work when the kids needed something. I was more important than him; therefore I could not possibly stay home. He was the one who took them to doctor appointments and stayed home if they were sick. He was the one who got up in the middle of the night. He contributed so significantly to every part of their life, so it made sense I would keep working, as I was not needed at home.

Now I had four healthy children. There were not many people in my past that would have believed the way my life unfolded. I could not believe it myself. There I was with my four little kids, living in my two million dollar house, with my big career, a new car every year, and being a big shot.

Scripture says, "It is easier for a camel to go through the eye of a needle than it is for a rich man to get to heaven[2]." You know why? Because when you are rich, it is easy to feel like you do not need God. You have everything.

God kept giving me blessing after blessing after blessing. I needed him but only kept pulling Him off the shelf and then putting Him back up again when I was done with Him.

Our fourth baby, another little girl, was just one month old on September 11, 2001...9/11. *What am I doing?* I thought. *What if I had died in those towers? What would happen to my kids? Would they even know me?* Suddenly, I realized how unimportant a job is compared to family. *I'm done,* I decided.

I walked into my boss's office and announced, "I quit!"

He leaned back and chuckled, shaking his head slowly. "Judy, people don't walk away from a job like this. You're experiencing post-partum depression. Go home and come back in eight weeks and do what you do best."

I stared at him and heard the words whispered on my heart: *I have bigger plans for you. Come follow me.* The reality of my vocation as wife and mother was stirring within me. I turned on my heels and walked out of that office.

I have never gone back to that industry and did not work for pay for the next seven years until I began speaking at events in 2009. The company continued to pay me commissions for five years thinking I would eventually be back. They did not think I could operate without the affirmation, the accumulation, the attainment, and the accomplishments that came with my career success.

It was at this point that I finally was able to really embrace

---

[2] Paraphrased from Matthew 19:24 and Mark 10:25

motherhood. It was the first time that I loved beyond myself in a way that I could feel and acknowledge. Ever. I had come a long way, but I still had further to go before I could stand to be in my own skin. Now I stood before four innocent children for whom I was completely responsible. It was very scary. I feared failing them, and that if I did, they would turn out like me.

I gave every ounce of energy I had to my children. There were no more nannies. I wanted to do it all, from driving, and cooking, to cheering the loudest at their sporting events. They became my entire world—my everything—and it felt so good to give them all of me. I was determined to be the best mother ever. After all, when I put my mind to something, it was never half way.

Chapter 7
Surrender

In 2003, Bob and I made a New Year's resolution to go back to church to "get God." The last time we had been in church was when we got married eleven years earlier. When I made that resolution, I went after it in the same way I had always done everything else...completely and fanatically. I signed up for everything.

Bob's idea of going back to church was simply "going to church." When he saw how fanatic I was becoming, he said, "You go ahead and do that; I'll see you on Sunday." So we did not exactly "get God" together.

Spiritually, we were on different wavelengths. My intentions were good—I wanted to please God. I read, studied, and learned about who God was, about the God of love, mercy, and forgiveness. My actions were about attaining God's approval, but through the process, I began to understand that I could trust Him. The more I learned, the more I loved. I could not get enough of Jesus. I learned that He was good and was forgiving, and He only allowed things out of love.

Then, on April 17, 2003, in the midst of throwing myself into religion, my life changed forever. The house of cards that I spent years building came crashing down in an instant. I found out that Bob had an affair in the past. There was a child. The woman had been demanding money from Bob, more and more all the time. Bob did not want me to find out, so his secret controlled him. It was a terrible, heavy burden with no escape.

Bob still loved me and he loved our children. He deeply regretted the affair and did not want our life together as a family to be over. He knew me well enough to expect the exact reaction that I had: divorce. And I was not one to change my mind once I made a decision.

Once I learned the truth, the marriage was over as far as I was concerned. I never would have believed Bob could have done something like this. It was a complete shock. Our life was shattered—completely, utterly, and irreparably broken into a million pieces. In its place was total brokenness. Rebuilding the wreckage seemed impossible and required more than I could comprehend. A gaping hole was all that was left.

I staggered around with a dazed sense of bewilderment, picking up the pieces that I judged were worthy of salvaging: my heart, my children, and my identity as a child of God. But not the marriage. That had to be over. I took the children for a little "vacation" to Florida to visit my parents for their approval to divorce Bob. From there, I would figure out what our next move would be.

That day I found out, I got on my knees and prayed the Magnificat and Divine Mercy Chaplet over and over. "Let it be done to me according to your will," I prayed reflecting the words of Our Blessed Mother. That, I believe, is when my real journey began. I emptied my broken heart of myself so now there was room for God.

Sometimes the only way the good Lord can get into some hearts is to break them." -Venerable Fulton Sheen.

I felt anger, self-pity, and despair. Yet, amazingly, the dominant feelings I had were grace and peace. It makes no sense rationally, but spiritually, that was what was happening. Never before had I known the cross could deliver me. Suddenly, I understood the way of the cross. This became the most profound time in my life, when I experienced Christ. My only solace and peace were in the Eucharist. I prayed, *Change me Lord, change me.*

The demise of my marriage was the pivotal point in my life. It was the beginning of a journey leading closer to God. As I decided to divorce, I was not afraid to be a single mother of four children all under the age of eight. I was, however, fearful of the judgment of others and looking like a failure as a wife. I went to my parents for their stamp of approval to divorce. They had just attended a World Wide Marriage Encounter weekend a few months earlier and had heard about Retrouvaille through the presenting couple.

"If you think your marriage is over, you have nothing to lose by going to a Retrouvaille weekend," my mother said. She pointed out that regardless of what happened to the marriage, since we had kids together, Bob and I should try to work out at least a cordial relationship and learn to communicate.

Since everything was already lost, I decided she was right— I had nothing more to lose by going. I committed to attending the weekend and post sessions. I wanted just one more piece of the wreckage to take with me on my journey as a single mother. There was never the slightest possibility in my mind that we would stay together. My goal was resolution to figure out how we would move on with four kids after the divorce.

Instead of it being the one last thing I did with Bob before I ended our marriage, Retrouvaille became a new beginning. It was the beginning of a lifelong journey of my personal transformation as well as that of our marriage. I made a decision to love, forgive, dialogue, and utilize the tools given to us that weekend.

Retrouvaille saved us. By the grace of God, we made the decision to love and forgive. There is hope and healing in God. Immediately upon making that decision, it was like an old broken faucet was suddenly fixed and turned on. Out poured mercy, forgiveness, and healing that in the past had just barely dripped out. My prayers now consisted of asking God for strength, acceptance, and grace to get through this.

I was forced to rewind and replay the events in my life. I saw my past as a world filled with anxiety, fear, insecurity, inadequacy, doubt, and pride. My excessive behaviors emulated those awful feelings: drugging, eating, exercising, and working were all part of running away.

I had been stripped of every part of who I thought I was and was ready to start the life-long process of transformation. The painful marriage crisis led me to God like never before. I had done everything in an attempt to gain affirmation, approval, and acceptance. "I accept, I am willing, and I am able to allow this challenge in my life," I prayed. Forgiveness and love were choices that I was now able and willing to make. I did not need to be blinded by anyone else's shortcomings; I could look at my own.

It was compassion without condemnation that allowed me freedom from judging my husband. I was not compelled to punish. I knew that as I judged, so I would be judged. I had faith that God's plan and purpose with this situation would help me to be a better person, better mother, and better wife. I did not worry about what might or might not happen. For once, I simply willingly followed God's lead.

True transformation took place for me that year and so did true love. Once I made the decision to forgive, the marriage, that I could not imagine surviving, thrived. Love blossomed anew.

Bob has the hardest time forgiving himself, and yet, he wants me to share this story and eventually came to tell our children what happened. It was not easy. When there is a child involved, the past is a part of the present and the future.

Bob is such an incredible husband and father. The only one who does not know how great he is, is him. We still struggle for Bob's lack of forgiveness of himself. He knows God forgives him and I forgive him, but he still struggles with his own forgiveness. Bob and I were able to rebuild our marriage, but we never forget that our children have another sibling and Bob has another daughter.

As I look back on that time when Bob kept the secret and it kept him, I considered how secrets cause us to hide. I also was not unfamiliar with hiding. In the Garden of Eden, Adam and Eve hid. But God always goes searching, "Where are you?" It is not because He doesn't know where we are; He wants *us* to know where we are.

Together, Bob and I can now stand united and give God all the glory. Because our children know, it was really like the ability to stand before them naked without shame. Here is where we are, here is where we have been, and there are no secrets. Bob and I can give tribute to each other and to God. We can tell our children, "Not many women would do what your mom has done—forgive and stay. Not many men would do what your dad has done to stay and fight." But they also understand that our determination and forgiveness was beyond our own abilities. It was the grace of God that gave us that ability to move forward and to truly love again.

Shattered people are hurt people, but there is nothing beyond God's ability to repair. True love is possible but it is not without pain. There is something very powerful in the brokenness that God's infinite mercy and grace can repair.

"And we know that God causes all things to work together for good to those who love God, to those who are called according to *His* purpose," (Romans 8:28).

When God repairs what is shattered, it becomes stronger. What once was bad can be renewed and be our strength. My history is my destiny. The very things that made me feel guilty and unworthy are the very things that God has taken to further His kingdom. To whom much is given much is expected. Those who are forgiven, forgive much. Those who are loved, love much. I was loved and forgiven by God. How could I not do the same for my husband?

I wanted to put a period at the end of our marriage, but God wanted to put a comma. It was like He said: *This story is not going to end this way. This is not going to end without Me being glorified.* His constant voice kept coming back to me: *I love you and I forgave you.*

When I had planned to divorce Bob, a friend said to me, "Until you love and forgive him the way God has loved and forgiven you, you cannot divorce him."

I had said, *No way!* I knew I did not love and forgive Bob the way God had loved and forgiven me. But then my heart was moved with pity. I knew what it is like to be living a lie and in so much pain. I know Bobby's heart, and I know that he is a good man and a Godly man. I did not know his heart then like I know it now. I know that he is sorry. There is nothing I could ever say that could make him more sorry than he already is.

I came to understand that you are not the only one that is in pain; your spouse is in pain too. The outside world does not look at it that way. Jesus shares in our suffering with us, just as a man and wife must shares in each other's sufferings rather than accusing and reminding the other of the past.

It is the message of the Church that we are forgiven. I am not saying there is not a tremendous need for the sacrament of Confession; it is transformative. God is not saving us without us. There's a collaborative effort, in, with, and through Jesus.

Bob says that he thinks about what happened every day. For myself, I can tell you there are days and weeks and it does not come to my mind. When it does come to mind, it is a reminder of what God did for our marriage. It is a feeling of greater gratitude and joy and the realization that what Satan used to try and destroy us, God used to save us.

JUDY HEHR
OVERCAME
DRUG ADDICTION
TO BECOME A
HEALTHY MOTHER
OF FOUR.

Chapter 8
Bob's Story

Judy speaks around the country, so her story and our marriage crisis and recovery are no secret. After her talks, people often wonder, "What about Bob? How does he feel about you sharing something so personal?" Or people come up to Judy and, in a whisper, share that they have traveled similar paths. Since I am not the speaker in the family, this is my opportunity to share my side of our marriage story.

I was born and raised in Bell Wood, Illinois, during the late 1960s and 70s, the middle of three children in a Presbyterian family. We went to church services around fifty percent of the time. Our family prayed sometimes and talked about God here and there, so He was a part of our lives. I did not really have much of a relationship with God, but I trusted that He was there.

My dad worked at a printing company, and my mom stayed home. We never had extra money when I was young, but we never went hungry. Chipped beef on toast or soup were common dinners as my parents lived frugally.

Dad was an alcoholic and a workaholic who eventually owned his own printing company. My parents sometimes fought about his drinking, especially when he came home late at night. At times there was tension, but divorce was never talked about. It was not so common back then. My dad was a wonderful father. He was sober the last five years of his life and died in 1998.

I consider my childhood to be happy with two loving parents. Neighborhood kids would assemble into teams to play whatever sport was in season using the street as our playground. We made sure to be home in time for dinner before running outside again and returning home for the night when the streetlights turned on.

My mom's parents had a cabin in Lake Geneva, Wisconsin, so as soon as school was out for summer, until it was time to go back, our family lived at the lake. My dad sometimes commuted the ninety-minute drive into Chicago, but usually we just saw him on weekends. During the winter, I skied most weekends at Lake Geneva. I was very close with my grandmother who spoiled me. She told me I could call her any time to come pick me up to go to the lake. Often, she picked me up right after school on Friday afternoons. I had my school friends and my Lake Geneva friends.

At age fifteen, I started working part-time at a steel company. The money was good back then, making $10 an hour in 1977. I went full-time after high school graduation.

I spent my money on wine, women, and song and, of course, a nice car. I had enough money to do what I wanted. Living the single life was beginning to wear on me just before I met Judy. Staying up late and going to parties every weekend was getting old.

I went to work at my dad's printing company when I was twenty-one. He taught me the ropes, rotating me around to the various jobs including sweeping, inventory, forklift driver, and finally both inside and outside sales. Our company sold printing supplies only to distributors. Judy worked for a distributor.

Her boss and my dad were good business friends. Judy's boss agreed to give my dad his business and, in turn, my dad treated his company like royalty.

Judy called one day with a question that my dad referred to me. I remembered her from a sales presentation I had done at her company. She did not seem to notice me at the time, but I definitely noticed her. Although most business could be handled over the phone, I suggested that we meet for lunch—to discuss business, of course.

Once business was handled, I asked Judy to go out with me to a Chicago Bulls game. It was back in the days of Michael Jordon. "I don't mix business with pleasure," she said.

"Well, this won't be business," I said.

"I don't drink and I don't do drugs, and if you do that, you should know I'm not into that," Judy told me.

I drank like a fish on the weekends. Judy had been in treatment in 1989, and we met in 1992. I was ready for a change.

"That's not a problem," I told her. After some persuasion, she accepted. We went with some friends of mine who later expressed surprise at the way I had acted with Judy. I held her hand and put my arm around her during the game. That was not something I usually did, especially on a first date. It felt so natural being with her.

After the game, we went out on the town for awhile and stayed with friends. Judy and I snuggled, listening to music and barely slept. I did not want to leave her so I hung around her the whole next day and watched football on TV. Later I found out she hated watching football on TV. From the time of our first date, I wanted to be with Judy as much as possible.

I was thirty years old and felt like a teenager in puppy love. I had met the perfect woman for me. Judy was fun, pretty, smart, witty, athletic, and had a good work ethic.

Our first date was November 5, 1992; we were engaged on January 9 and married on August 28, 1993. As my eighty-year-old grandmother said when I first excitedly told her about Judy, "When you know, you will know." We both knew.

I married the woman of my dreams, and we honeymooned for a

week in Hawaii. We had twenty-two months together alone before our first baby, Carter, was born. Life was good. We made a lot of money between us, had a new house, a country club membership, nice cars, and we spent almost every weekend in Lake Geneva. Adding a baby was the icing on the cake.

I think I adjusted better than Judy. Her career was so demanding that it was harder for her. We had a nanny because Judy worked seventy to eighty hours a week, and I worked around ten hours a day.

I would relieve the babysitter because I knew Judy would not be there. My dad offered me a promotion, but I did not take it because I needed to be responsible for my wife and little boy. My wife was making ten times what I was making, so it was not up for discussion. It was an understanding with us, and I did not feel resentful.

Eighteen months later, Chandler, another boy, was born. It was the same routine. Even with babies, we still managed to go to Lake Geneva every weekend where we also had built-in babysitters with my parents. Kennedy, our first daughter, was born twenty-two months later. Having three children threw me for a loop because Kennedy was colicky, which meant I was not getting much sleep at night. Judy was never around.

Even on the delivery table she would be on the phone with a customer. Judy usually returned to work within a few days.

Thirty-five months later, Kampbell, a girl, was born. It was before our fourth baby that I had an affair. I met this person through work. Judy and I had become two ships passing in the night. She was never home, and when she got home, she was so tired, she was out cold the minute she hit the pillow.

I have a daughter from the affair. She was born before our daughter Kampbell was born in August of 2001. The woman wanted more money all the time. The final demand for money was the breaking point. I confided in Judy's brother and he told her. I was at home with the kids and Judy called me on the house phone in April of 2003.

"Keep the babysitter there and meet me at my sister's house and leave now," she said. My gut was wrenching. She knew. When I arrived, Judy called me every name in the book. "We are done!" she cried. "Our marriage is over!"

I was devastated. No way did I want the marriage to end. *What have I done?* I cried. Guilt and shame filled me. Judy was filled with anger and hated what I had done. We both cried.

Judy took the kids to Florida and told her Dad we were done. As far as the kids knew, they were taking a vacation. Judy's mother said, "You know Judy, I totally understand how you feel, but Dad and I were just at a Marriage Encounter weekend and heard about this ministry for troubled marriages called Retrouvaille. You are going to have to deal with Bob and have to communicate, so you might as well go."

We went two weeks later in May 2003. I wanted to reconcile, but I did not think in a million years that it was going to happen. Judy and I had been married for ten years, and I knew that when she puts her mind to something that is it.

Judy stared out the window for the entire ninety-minute drive on the way to the Retrouvaille weekend. She was heartbroken. Ironically, we had just made a New Year's resolution that previous January 2003 to start going to church. Neither of our daughters was baptized at that time.

Judy does not do anything halfway. After resolving to "get God," she started going over and beyond just Sunday Mass. She read every book about faith and was reading the Bible and going to daily Mass. Judy was no longer working then, because after 9/11 hit, she decided to make her family a priority.

When I pulled into the parking lot, couples that volunteered after having been through the weekend greeted us. Retrouvaille is a whole weekend event from Friday until Sunday afternoon.

I saw the face of God in the people who greeted us. We are friends with them to this day. By Saturday night, Judy and I made a decision to love and try to make it work. It was not easy. Judy wanted every question answered.

I have never seen that child. The woman got married, and I gave up my parental rights. We sought Godly counsel about this. I had little children at the time and did not want them to know about it.

For two years, Judy cried every day. She was heartbroken that I could have done this to her. After two years, I went to her dad and said, "I don't know how long I can take this." Her Dad told me, "The day she stops crying is the day that you're done."

Through the pain and through our healing, Judy and I fell in love again. After Retrouvaille, our love grew much deeper. We understand love now, and it does not compare to what we thought love was in the beginning.

For the first ten years, we had every material thing but our life fell apart. Now we have less money than we have ever had, and we are happier than we ever were. We also learned how to communicate. Once, we did not communicate well except on the surface, but now we can talk with each other about everything on a deeper level.

In Retrouvaille, we do not know anyone who has gone through what Judy and I have, where there is a child. With an affair, it is in your past, but with a child, it is your past, present, and future.

I was hoping that I would never have to tell my kids, but the time came when I felt I needed to let them know. They have all heard it from me at different ages. Telling my kids was a very powerful thing for me to do. Once they knew, they said that the way we parent them makes sense. They know about Judy's and my past and know that we do not want them to make the same mistakes.

I wanted our family to be one of faith, and I came to understand the importance of a relationship with God. I enrolled in RCIA classes (Right of Christian Initiation of Adults) in 2003 and became Catholic in 2005. When I had no one to turn to, Jesus was my best friend. The affair was not something that you would want to share about with your friends.

While I was learning the Catholic faith, I had a great teacher in Judy. She was enrolled in the seminary from 2004 to 2008. She studied so much and could answer all my questions, so it became something else we could talk about and be excited about.

Our faith had a lot to do with our healing. Judy was eager to learn and she does everything full blast, including sharing her story now to glorify God and help others. People often wonder, *Does it make you uncomfortable?* The answer is—a little. But I spoke about it at a Retrouvaille weekend around six years ago and realized that sharing it could help others.

I am glad that Judy talks about it. If she was not able to talk about it, I do not think that she would be able to be with me. The fact that it still makes me uncomfortable that it happened is because I will always be sorry about it, but it no longer controls me. Any time Judy or I talk about it, it is freeing and healing and cleansing, and it is an opportunity to help others.

Chapter 9
Kids' Perspective

I am Carter Hehr, the oldest son of Judy and Bob Hehr. Upon graduating from the University of Arizona, I took a job as a Zimmer Biomet surgical sales associate in Scottsdale.

Growing up, I thought I had or could get anything I wanted. By no means was I the stereotypical "spoiled rich kid," but I definitely did not have much adversity as a young boy. We lived in a 10,000 square foot house from the time I was three until eight years old. However, I did not think much of it because it was the "typical" house in the subdivision we lived in. I remember being envious of the neighbors who had pools and full court basketball courts in their backyard; all I had was a swing set and a lot of grass.

During my childhood, we went through a lot of babysitters. Both my parents worked full time until I was in junior high. We went through babysitters like clockwork. I cannot confirm whether that is a result the behavior of my brother' and I, or the babysitter doing a poor job.

When I was five years old, my brother, who was two years younger, and I did everything together. One story I remember is that we did not like a babysitter because she would not let us do what we wanted—typical for a three and five-year-old to be upset about something like that. We rode off on our bikes so the babysitter would chase after us. We proceeded to hide in a neighbor's yard, waiting for her to run past looking for us. Once she ran past, we ran back to the house and locked her out. My mom was working in her home office that day and wanted to know where the babysitter was and why we were in her office. The babysitter was locked out. I am not 100% sure, but I think we had a new babysitter days later.

My mom was gone a lot. That being said, when she was with us, she did everything she could to make up for being gone so much. I did not think anything of her being gone a lot for two reasons. First, it was all I knew, and second, we had a playroom with endless toys above our four-car garage.

I loved my childhood because we got just about everything we wanted. Sometimes it took convincing and begging. My mom and dad were probably so annoyed with our persistence that they said *yes* just to shut us up. We were extremely well behaved, and I remember my parents never allowing tantrums or whining. They were strict about being on our best behavior, especially in public. Now that I am twenty-two, I can see than although we got a lot that we wanted, we were raised to be thankful, respectful, and by no means "better" than anyone.

After 9/11, my mom realized that the only way she could be more involved in our lives was by not working. She is someone who does not do anything half way; it is always a 150% effort. I thought it would be great to have her around more, but by sixth, seventh, and eighth grade, I felt she was *over* involved. Although we are very close now, at the time, I did not want my mom attempting to control me like a puppet.

I remember going on a vacation to Florida and having no idea that my mom was planning on divorcing my dad. We were protected from their issues completely, and although we were nine years old and younger, neither of them tried to play us against the other.

During the teen years, I often fought with my parents, especially during high school. I was a good kid— not perfect—but I had multiple other parents tell me they wished I were their son. Which I, of course, told my parents with the end goal of them loosening up. They were extremely overprotective and attempted to micromanage everything.

Out of no-where, we started doing community service on holidays and praying at night and before meals. We even went to church every

Sunday. Like I said before, my mom does not do things halfway. It was all the way or not at all.

I wanted to know, "Why is Sunday all of a sudden about church and God?"

"You don't *have* to go to church, you *get* to go," my parents would say. "This is something that is extremely important to have God in your life."

I had everything that I wanted growing up without religion, so I did not understand why we needed to add one more thing. I was under the impression that we were doing pretty good without God.

I went to public school from kindergarten until fifth grade. Middle school came, and all of a sudden, I was sent to the Catholic school. I went to Catholic school for all of middle school then switched back to public school for high school. The Catholic school was twenty minutes away compared to five minutes away for the public school. The longer drive made the Catholic school an inconvenience for me.

During middle school, once I was educated on the subject of religion, I began to realize its importance. Being surrounded with faith-based people and kids my age, I started to understand "God" and "church every Sunday." Gradually, I went from apathy to understanding the commandments, and the entire Catholic faith.

After high school, I went to the University of Arizona and played division one football. I was beyond ecstatic to get away from my parents at that point. I was eighteen and ready to be on my own. While I was at school, my mom sent me inspirational quotes every day. I had promised her that I would send her "my strongest feeling" for the day for forty days. They were typically feelings that had to do with my emotions toward playing football at the time. (She sent me quotes all through college and still does to this day.)

After freshman year, I had a two-week summer break before having to be back for football. I had not seen my friends from high school in over a full year. My first thought was that I had to party with them. One night after drinking and partying at a friend's house, I came home late, went to bed, and got up for work the next morning. While I was at work as a boat driver parking boats at a marina, my mom showed up. She drove all the way down to the launch ramp, and in front of my friends, she gave me the dirtiest look and said, "Get in the car. You're coming home." As we drove off, she yelled to my boss and said, "Carter will be taking the rest of the day off."

This is insane! I thought. Before even leaving the parking lot, she was telling me that I smelled like booze. Like any other teenager who would not want to be in trouble or have to deal with his parents, I lied and said, "I didn't drink." I was underage drinking, but I did not think too much of it, considering I spent my freshman year at the University of Arizona. When I got home, my dad was sitting at the kitchen counter. Both of my parents were upset with me, and I was upset with them for treating me like a child.

"I can do what I want!" I told them. "I'm in college now!" They threatened to call my head football coach, Rich Rodriguez, and tell him that I did not care about the opportunity he gave me to play football at Arizona.

They yelled at me about how I was ruining my life, and I sat there, hung-over, not letting what they were saying get to me. All of a sudden, they both started crying. My dad said, "Is it the time to tell him?" My mom nodded.

"Carter," he said. "I'm going to tell you something right now that may explain a lot." He pointed to a painting that was above the fireplace. The painting included my brother and two sisters and me at the beach. On the beach laid a starfish.

"Do you know what that starfish stands for?" Dad asked with tears in his eyes.

"No," I said, confused at why he was starting to cry.

He proceeded to tell me that he had a kid with another woman during my parent's marriage. It completely changed the mood. I realized why they were so strict about everything relating to lying, cheating, or stealing. It *all* made sense now. I sat at the kitchen counter with uncontrollable tears streaming down my face. My dad explained that he was strict with us because he did not want us to make mistakes that would hurt us or our future.

"I've wanted something more for you," he said. Dad was very apologetic and explained that his bad decision is something that affects him on a daily basis and almost separated my parents.

I was aware something happened when I was growing up. They referenced there was an issue of the past and now I knew what it was. I thought it had something to do with money, but I had no idea it was an affair.

I realized the magnitude of how one mistake can change your life. I shifted my emotion. The first words that came out of my mouth were, "You guys are proof true love exists." I looked at my Dad, crying his eyes out, and hugged him and thanked him for all he has done. I can only imagine what he had to do to make things right and the sacrifices he made for our family.

I am extremely close with my parents now. I felt closer to them both at that moment than probably ever before. We ended up talking for hours. They answered all of my questions. That was four years ago.

That day marked a permanent change in our relationship—a new understanding, a new respect for who they were and what they wanted for us. It has also changed how I look at marriage. I have a greater respect for marriage as a result of this and realize how important it is to never give up. I thank God daily for what He did in my parents' life and how that drastically changed my life.

I am grateful my parents stayed together. They are an example of what "fighting for the one you love" and forgiveness is all about.

* * * * * *

I am Kennedy Hehr, the first girl and third child of Bob and Judy Hehr. I am currently nineteen years old and a student athlete attending Coastal Carolina University.

When I was a little girl, I was always daddy's little girl. Whenever my mom would come in my room when I was a baby or toddler, my response was always, "Get out, and get Dad." It did not matter the circumstance; I wanted my dad there. I do not know if that was because my mom was never around or what the reasoning was. My mom was never home because she was working 24/7 making money and supporting the family; it was the same with my dad though. That is the exact reason why my siblings and I got just about anything that we wanted as children, because my parents worked so hard for that to be possible. I know for a fact that both of my parents worked the way they did for their children, not for themselves. To this day, my parents live for us kids. They may live for us way too much sometimes, but that is because they do not want us to make the mistakes they did.

Something I will never forget is that no matter how much money my parents brought in, they always knew how blessed we were, and they were not defined by their success. Although we lived a lifestyle in the top one percent, there were always boundaries and expectations and never a sense of entitlement. I do not think people would have known how much money we had back then. That is a direct reflection of the way my parents raised us, and I am forever grateful for it.

When I was in second grade, my parents moved us to a Catholic school, and we all graduated eighth grade from there. We went to church every Sunday and my parents were present at every school Mass. From First Communion in second grade to Confirmation my senior year, I grew tremendously in my faith. After learning for many years about what life is like when you are active in your faith, I wanted nothing more than to do that. From setbacks to comebacks, I can testify that all things are possible with God. Another thing that I constantly thank my parents for is showing us the importance of having a relationship with God, because that is truly something that has changed my life.

Throughout middle school at St. Francis de Sales, I watched and listened to constant bickering between my oldest brother, Carter, and my parents. I always wondered why in the heck they were all over him for every little thing he did. I got to high school and it was a complete shock. Girls just hand over their dignity like it's nothing? Guys lie like crazy just to get what they want from a girl? Friends are only there when times are good? The answer to all those questions is *yes*, which is quite brutal. My parents were on my back as well. It felt like every little thing I did was watched, and then I was told it was wrong.

I am one of the few girls these days that seems to have true respect for herself. Not only because my parents wanted that for me, but also because I wanted it for myself. I take tremendous pride in that. Anyway, it was as if nothing was ever good enough for my parents. I would say to them, "You should be thanking me for the teenager that I am because the choices I make are not even close to as bad as what everyone else does." They would respond, "We don't care, that's the bare minimum. You aren't like everyone else." I am not going to lie when I say that they being all up in my business, all the time, was beyond annoying. Privacy was not necessarily a thing in the Hehr house. I never understood why they were so protective and over the top, but after hearing their story, it all made sense.

One day at school, I got a text from my mom saying she and my dad needed to talk to me that night. I remember sitting in the chair in the living room while my mom was on the couch and my dad was at the island. Above the fireplace was a painting of my three siblings and me on a beach, with a starfish in the corner.

My parents made eye contact, and my mom went on to explain that there was an affair and my dad had another child. She explained the symbolism of the starfish. They both started bawling their eyes out.

My mom asked me what mattered most to me, and I responded with,

"Dad is here. That is what matters. I have more respect for him because of that than he thinks." I had never seen my dad cry so hard in his life, besides after my car accident, which I barely remember. He was a wreck, and he did not want any of his kids to ever be in a situation like that. "The present will someday be in your past, but your past will always be present in your future." That is a saying my mom always tells us.

Up until my parents told me their story, I never knew the reasoning behind her saying that. One decision can really change your life forever. After they explained things to me and answered the few questions I had, all the pieces started to come together in my head. Retrouvaille and the grace of God saved my parents' marriage. But if they did not do the things they did to fight for their love, they would not be where they are today, and neither would our family. I am beyond grateful for the role that God played in my family's life. I have always had a strong faith, and my parents' story strengthened it even more.

Once all of us kids knew, it changed our lives. The amount of respect we all have for our parents is insane because of what they did. I cannot even imagine the sacrifices they had to make and the struggles they had to go through to keep our family connected.

I thank God for the way He worked through our family. My parents are an example of how true love really can fight through anything and how God can intervene in anyone's life. Just like when I was a child, I will always be my dad's "little girl," no matter what the past consisted of.

Christmas 2002

Christmas 2003

Christmas 2004

Christmas 2005

Christmas 2006

Christmas 2008

Christmas 2009

Christmas 2016

Chapter 10
Abandonment

My marriage crisis initially involved all five of my siblings, as they were made aware of the details surrounding the divorce that was going to be forthcoming. They also were affected by the way I chose to navigate my change of heart to reconcile with Bob. Unfortunately, I felt it best at the time to focus only on my marriage and four children, and to distance our family entirely from my siblings. In an attempt to enlighten them to what was happening in my life, my marriage, and my heart, I wrote them a letter. The situation with my marriage had some long-term effects on my relationships with my siblings.

I will share excerpts from that letter hoping to convey how important it was to me for them to understand the revelations I had, that I was embracing this cross as a gift from God, and how it was that I believed that Bob and I could move forward.

Today I write about the many revelations I've experienced since my life was changed on April 17. The whirlwind of the past two and half months is incredible...

Through much prayer, thought, reading, and soul-searching, I have taken in a wealth of newfound information and feel a real understanding of my life, my present circumstances and myself. Since April 17, my daily prayer has consisted of asking God for the strength, acceptance, willingness, and grace to get through this period of my life.

The present set of circumstances lead me to be driven to God like never before. The vengeance in which I pursued filling the hole in my soul is now used in my pursuit of peace and contentment through a relationship with God. The humility bestowed upon me has brought awareness, strength, and the ability to see my responsibility in this life....

I am willing and able to accept this challenge in my life as a blessing. God's way of revealing His unfailing love in the midst of total darkness is nothing short of a miracle.... I have been stripped of every part of who I thought I was and am ready to start the lifelong process of transformation. I hope to be molded into a new person who thinks and behaves in a way that pleases God above all else. The cross I have been given to bear has allowed me to want something entirely different than before....

As far as my family is concerned, I feel the changes I have made will help them build a better sense of security. They will have a better example to emulate...The very thing that brought their parents together must keep them united in trying to rebuild what has begun to deteriorate through this situation and the past ten years without spirituality.

I hope to also show by my action and words that the love I have for my siblings is absolute. I feel blessed today that each of my siblings was brought into this.They have each had a significant piece to add to my journey from despair to hope.

You have all been so important to me in so many different ways at different times in my life. I treasure each of you and want you in my family's life. I pray we can get through this together and grow to love each other despite our differences. I know it may take time, but I pray that you will also be able to let go of your negative feelings and let God handle the rest I love you all!

Somewhere in the course of this journey of faith I was given a renewed mind. It did not think the way it used to think. I am living proof of what God can do to a mind and heart if someone comes to Him and says, "Change me. Help me *believe* who You say I am. Help me to *become* who You say I am."

Looking back while writing this book, I continue to be amazed at the countless ways God has restored, renewed, and pursued every aspect of my mind, body, and spirit. I asked two old friends what their perspectives had been of me back in the day. I would never have described me this way, yet perception is reality and this was theirs.

Here is what Mary Kay Bartelt, my best friend from high school who saw me fall apart after my mother died and even encouraged me to get help, who is a friend to this day shared with me:

> Judy's struggle with and eventual survival and thriving over her drug disease is amazing and a true miracle. She was always such a funny, positive, and encouraging person. I was drawn to that when we first met, however, her descent into the use of drugs and associating with less than stellar characters, took a big toll on her personality as well as her life. This was especially difficult for me being her roommate. I bore the brunt of her mood swings and sometimes-erratic behavior. She was quick to anger and could be unpredictable. Something that could send her into a rage and slamming doors one day would go unnoticed the next.
>
> It was a very confusing and difficult environment in which to live. Judy started having issues with honesty, lying, and even theft, as she needed to support her addiction. I think the part that was hardest to witness was her total lack of self-worth. She believed that she was garbage, and she treated herself as such.
>
> Thankfully, Judy's story has a positive, happy ending, unlike so many others…. It was wonderful to see her put her efforts into something that turned out to be so positive for her. She is now centered, whole, and lives her life with dignity. She has a calm and serene presence that is not easily rattled. She tries to live out her faith to the best of her ability without being hyper-judgmental, hypocritical, or shaming. Sometimes when people "find God" they can make others uncomfortable, and you don't want to be around them a lot because they're always preaching, proselytizing, or trying to convert. That is not the case with Judy. She makes you want some of what she has.

What a great example for our Church. And let me add that our Church needs some great examples right now.

* * * * * *

Although I tend to remember very little from my school years, a friend Kathy shared her perspective of me from sixth to eighth grade.

You were a competitive girl in sports and friends and boys. You were loyal to those who were loyal to you. You were both self-deprecating while also poking fun at others, though sometimes a little rough. You were funny and playful and wild. You enjoyed attention. As a leader, you pushed back on authority, which gave us permission to do so, too. You seemed fearless most of the time. I wish I still had all the notes that we passed back then.

That's how I remember you, my friend. The cool boys thought you were cool. The shy boys probably thought you were crazy. The cool girls weren't intimidated by you. The shy girls probably were. The teachers probably had differing views depending on their age and tolerance.

One word to describe you would have been auspicious.

* * * * * *

It has been fifteen years since my marriage crisis unfolded. Since then, my faith and reality have intersected with our Catholic theology.

One year later, in 2004, I was a sponge for my ongoing conversion and Catholic faith. It was suggested by the director of our religious education program that I should apply to the seminary. That seemed outrageous to me. She took the time to help me with my application and recommendation. I applied and was accepted into a ministry formation program at the St. Francis de Sales Seminary in Milwaukee. Who would have predicted that? I certainly did not think I would be accepted. I had no formal college education, no ministerial or pastoral experience, and I was inactive and away from the church for twenty years. Yet, at this time, my desire to know, love, and serve God had become the reason I existed.

When I went there, I was an outsider. I did not look like, act like, or pray like those in my class. I was one of thirty-three others, and the only one who did not work in the Church in some capacity. They were as surprised as I was that I was there. I heard things like, "How did you get in?"

Initially, I could not answer that question. However, I came to believe that it was God in His infinite love and mercy that orchestrated this entire situation for my highest and best good. After a few years, I knew that I was supposed to be there, and it was the most transformational time of my faith journey.

"God invited me in," I would say. "I am the one Jesus left the gate open for. I was lost and am the last sheep!"

For the first two years in seminary, it was my perception that my peers did not embrace me. They represented the Church to me, and that was very troubling. The temptation to feel less than, to feel unworthy, was nearly overwhelming. But God chose me to be in that place at that time. I was excited to learn everything I could about my God and my faith, so I could pass on this gift of faith to my husband and children.

My time spent in seminary was part of a formation program, and by the end, I was formed into the image and likeness of my Lord. I not only learned about God, I learned to love Him, to depend on Him, and about His love for me. As I fell in love with my faith, I also fell more in love with my husband. God had this planned for me; it was all for good.

God kept changing my heart through the dying and rising of everything I thought my life was supposed to be. Everything I had originally believed my marriage would be did not turn out that way. Everything I thought my family would be did not turn out that way. Everything I thought I was and would be

88

certainly did not turn out that way. I had to realize that *it's not about me; it's about God.* And God had a much bigger plan for me.

I experienced physical and emotional healing, but after those two—which seem to be the worst and almost unbearable when you are going through it—comes spiritual healing. That is the life-changing part. That is the part that makes it last. That is the part where God puts together all the shattered pieces of my broken heart and sets it apart, into a new formation in His image.That happened for me. Somewhere along the way, I learned that all excess is rooted in emptiness.

Scripture tells us, "Love the Lord your God with all your heart, with all your mind, with all your strength – and love your neighbor as yourself.[3]" No half-hearted lovers for this God. And that last phrase about loving your neighbor *as yourself?* How do you possibly love your neighbor? How do you possibly love your God if the end statement is not coming into fruition within the core of your being? Loving yourself?

It is out of love for God that you can love yourself and that you can love your neighbor. When all I had left was God to turn to, God to talk to, God to love, *then I got it.*

I have dealt with addictions to people, drugs, alcohol, food, cigarettes, shopping, success, and exercise—and I had to be willing to lay down my crown. My mouth has always been bigger than my heart, and I lived a life that was prayer-less and therefore powerless. I made more than my share of mistakes, and I do not claim to be perfect, but I know that God truly loves me the way I am--imperfections and all.

I desire to be the best wife I can be to my husband. I choose to love him unconditionally. My journey is one of image and likeness as I seek to be Christ to my husband and for my husband; to allow him to see Christ in me, in all my words, and all my actions.

---

[3] Found in the Gospels of Matthew (22:37), Mark (12:30), and Luke (10:27)

I desire to be the best mother I can be to my children. They will probably have a long list of things I have done wrong and could have (should have) done better, but I will have been successful if they know who and whose they are and the love that God has for them. It is one of my greatest desires that they know they too are chosen, adopted, redeemed, and forgiven.

You have heard that "God does not call the qualified; He qualifies the called." Clearly I am not qualified to be where I am based on my credentials or my faithfulness to God. But this I know: it is God's way of revealing His unfailing love in the midst of darkness. I can forgive because I have been forgiven; I can show mercy because mercy has been given to me. And I can love because I have been loved by a God who makes all things possible for those who believe in Him.

There is a Scripture verse that says, "He who began a good work in you will bring it to completion[4]." I am so far from completion, and I realize that. I am not what I should be, but I am definitely not who I was. I do not believe it was a coincidence that God's Word came to fruition in my life at age thirty-seven and four months! One of my favorite Psalms today is Psalm 37:4. I finally delighted in the Lord and He gave me the desires of my heart. I have had the gift of a privileged perspective of my God, my life, and myself. Today I continue living in God's Word and being the active change I want to be in my family, in my community, and in my world. I hope. I know for sure I do not stand a chance without God's grace. I know. I tried that. I also know that it is not enough to believe *in* Him; you have to *believe* Him. If you don't accept His forgiveness, then He died in vain, which He definitely did not!

I am Judy Hehr. I am: Wife to Bob; Mother to Carter, Chandler, Kennedy, and Kampbell.

---

[4] Philippians 1:6

I believe my history to be my destiny.
I have lived in captivity. I have lived in liberty.
God has turned my misery into ministry.

I have a story to tell that might bring some hope.
I was bankrupt at 20, a *millionaire* at 30,
Single, homeless, drug addicted at 22, a *healthy* mother of four at 34,
College dropout at 22, a seminary *graduate* at 42,
Scorned, broken, almost divorced at 37, *sanctified* in a thriving marriage today.

However, my true identity is found in the fact that I can stand before you today and tell you that I am a beloved child of God.

The home our children grew up in

I pray you were blessed by
reading about Gods infinite
love mercy and grace.

Your prayers for this ministry
and my family are appreciated

Contact information

www.judyhehr.com

f /judyhehr

◎ /hehrjudy

𝕏 /hehrjudy

You Tube /judy.hehr

✉ judy@mydynamicdirection.com

CPSIA information can be obtained
at www.ICGtesting.com
Printed in the USA
FSHW021458220220
67318FS

9 780692 962312